SCHOOL-WIDE GUIDANCE: BE A

Quick And Easy Programs To Motivate Every Student

Grades K-6

**WRITTEN BY
Lisa Miller**

Cover and coloring contest illustrations by Jeffrey Zwartjes

Lisa Miller

Lisa Miller is a K-6 elementary counselor with the Midview Local School District in Grafton, Ohio. Before assuming her present position, she worked as a family/consumer science teacher. Mrs. Miller is an adjunct professor at Ashland University and a PRAXIS III® new-teacher assessor for the Ohio Department of Education.

An established author, she has developed several publications for Mar*co Products, including:

Meaningful Motivators
Stress-Less Bingo
Who Is Your School Counselor?

Lisa lives in Lorain, Ohio with her husband Dave, their son Austin, dog Meggie, and two cats, Rusty and Reggie.

SCHOOL-WIDE GUIDANCE: BE A SHINING STAR!

10-DIGIT ISBN:1-57543-150-5   13-DIGIT ISBN: 978-1-57543-150-5

GRAPHIC DESIGN/LAYOUT: Cameon Funk

COPYRIGHT © 2007 MAR*CO PRODUCTS, INC.
Published by mar*co products, inc.
1443 Old York Road
Warminster, PA 18974
1-800-448-2197
www.marcoproducts.com

PERMISSION TO REPRODUCE: The purchaser may reproduce the activity sheets, free and without special permission, for participant use for a particular group or class. Reproduction of these materials for an entire school system is forbidden.

All rights reserved. Except as provided above, no part of this book may be reproduced or transmitted in whole or in part in any form or by any means, electronic or mechanical, including photocopying, recording, or by any information storage or retrieval system without permission in writing by the publisher.

PRINTED IN THE U.S.A.

CONTENTS

INTRODUCTION 6
   Shining Star Guidance 6
   Monthly School-Wide Activities 7
   Instructions For Using The CD 7

SHINING STAR GUIDANCE PROGRAM 9
   Game Plan 1 10
      Shining Star Student Nomination Forms 12
      Shining Star Certificate 13
   Game Plan 2 14
      Shining Star Guidance In A Bag Flyer (Sample) 16
      Shining Star Guidance In A Bag Flyer 17
   Game Plan 3 18
      Shining Star Convenient Times Flyer 20
      Shining Star Reads Schedule 21
      Shining Star Reads Reminder Slips 22
   Game Plan 4 23
      Suggested Words Of The Month/Character Traits List 25
      Shining Star Video/DVD Service Flyer 26
      Shining Star Video/DVD Schedule 27
   Game Plan 5 28
      Shining Star Nomination Form 30
      Shining Star Recording Paper 31
      Shining Star Certificate 32
   Game Plan 6 33
      Shining Star Checkup Slips 34
   Game Plan 7 39
      Word Of The Month Coloring Sheets 41
      Word Of The Month Coloring-Contest Winner Certificate 53
   Game Plan 8 57
      Shining Star Poster Contest Sheet 59
      Shining Star Character Trait Of The Month Poster Winner 60
   Game Plan 9 61
      Suggested Bingo Games 62
      Dine-And-Discuss Luncheon Parents' Invitation 64
      Dine-And-Discuss Luncheon Evaluation 65
   Game Plan 10 66
      Suggested Games 67
      Referral Form 68
      Notification Form 69

SHINING STAR MONTHLY SCHOOL-WIDE GUIDANCE PROGRAMS 71

Game Plan 1 For School-Wide Guidance (September) 72
- How To Have A Successful School Year For You And Your Child Flyer 74
- How Well Do You Know _____ School? Game Directions For Play 75
- Point Value Cards 76
- Game Headers 77
- How Well Do You Know _____ School? Game Questions And Answers 83

Game Plan 2 For School-Wide Guidance (October) 86
- Red Ribbon Week Flyer 87
- Red Ribbon Week Teacher Instructions 88
- "Hug Not Drugs" Day Coupons 89

Game Plan 3 For School-Wide Guidance (November) 90
- Bye, Bye, Bully Situation Cards 92
- Bye, Bye, Bully Invitation Flyer 94

Game Plan 4 For School-Wide Guidance (December) 95
- Caring Candles Instructions 96
- Caring Candle Activity Sheet 97

Game Plan 5 For School-Wide Guidance (January) 98
- Academic Responsibility Awards Nomination Form 100
- Academic Shining Stars Reporting Form 101
- Certificate Of Academic Responsibility 102
- Academic Excellence Certificate 107
- High Honor Roll Certificate 108
- Merit Roll Certificate 109

Game Plan 6 For School-Wide Guidance (February) 110
- It's National School Counselors' Week 111
- It's National School Counselors' Week Drawing Cards 112
- It's National School Counselors' Week Prize List 113

Game Plan 7 For School-Wide Guidance (March) 114
- In Your Own Words… 115

Game Plan 8 For School-Wide Guidance (April) 121
- Staff Alert For Ducky Day! 123
- Duck Pattern 124

Game Plan 9 For School-Wide Guidance (May) 125
- Thank You Cards 126

Dedication

To Him
who helps me help others.

INTRODUCTION

1,200 STUDENTS, 1 SCHOOL COUNSELOR. How many of you began your school counseling career in the face of comparable or even greater odds? Most of you reading this book can probably relate to the difficulties these overwhelming odds create, due to your responsibility to counsel a large number of students, improve the scope and efficacy of counseling services, and, above all, "fix what's wrong."

At the start of my school counseling career, I shuttled back and forth between two buildings each day, trying to serve approximately 1,200 K-3 students. And when I didn't think it could get any more hectic, my job description was expanded to servicing three buildings and counseling a whopping 2,000 children in Grades K-6. I have often wondered, "What in the world have I gotten myself into?" I'd had a high school teaching job with one prep period a day, teaching approximately 100 young people. Like most high school teachers, I had no idea what it would be like to interact with the same 30 kids all day, every day. I soon learned to appreciate and admire the elementary school teacher and the taxing job he or she does.

When I decided to move from high school to elementary, I soon realized I was expected to be in 20 different places at once. I had to come up with a plan. And fast. This book is my plan. It includes many of the programs I developed in order to provide meaningful guidance for 2,000 students. Each of these programs has proved very effective during the course of my career, and I hope they will inspire you to try something different, provide encouragement if you are struggling with a particular concept or problem, or be just what you have been looking for.

SHINING STAR GUIDANCE

School-Wide Guidance: Be A Shining Star! is designed to increase positive social interaction among children in Grades K-6. In other words, to put a stop to the day-to-day bullying, teasing, and fighting that take up much of a counselor's time. In the *Shining Star Guidance* program, students learn character skills that are essential to healthy social interaction. These skills involve making positive choices; respecting others; being responsible; showing compassion; learning to be fair, honest, and cooperative; practicing good citizenship; and developing self-esteem.

MONTHLY SCHOOL-WIDE ACTIVITIES

This book also includes school-wide activities for nine months. These easily planned activities benefit many students and parents without taking up a lot of time.

The book is divided into 19 game-plan strategies. Today's educators are looking for ways to keep students interested in learning and in staying in school. To realize these goals, school must become a place where students want to be. The 19 game-plan strategies in this book are designed to appeal to every student and may motivate students to leave school at the end of the day exclaiming, "Do you know what we're doing in school this month?"

INSTRUCTIONS FOR USING THE CD

The *School-Wide Guidance* reproducible pages are provided in two formats—black and white pages or color PDF files (found on the included CD, back inside cover).

System requirements to open PDF (.pdf) files:
Adobe Reader® 5.0 or newer (compatible with Windows 2000® or newer or Mac OS 9.0® or newer).

These files offer the user color versions of the reproducible pages found in the book. For example: *013_schoolwideguid.pdf* is the same as page 13 in the book.

These files cannot be modified/edited.

Shining Star

GUIDANCE PROGRAM

GAME PLAN 1

WHO:

Students in grades K-6

WHAT: SHINING STAR CELEBRITY CLUB

Each week, teachers nominate students for performing good deeds that demonstrate understanding of a specific character trait. The *Shining Star Celebrity Club* recognizes 20 of these students each week by giving each one a small reward for becoming a *Shining Star Student.*

PROGRAM IN ACTION:

Students will have many chances every day to earn a *Shining Star.* Students might earn a *Shining Star* by helping another child, getting an *A* on a paper, turning homework in on time, returning lost money, etc.

> Example: A student returns lost lunch money he/she found in the hallway. The teacher fills out a *Shining Star Nomination* form for the student. Then the child goes to the office and deposits the slip in the *Shining Star Treasure Chest.*

Each Tuesday, the counselor will draw the names of 20 students from the *Shining Star Treasure Chest*. He/she records the names drawn and, during Friday-morning announcements, introduces these students as the *Shining Stars* of the week. The selected students go to the office when their names are called, and each one receives a *Shining Star Certificate*, a special treat (or other reward), and a pencil.

WHEN:

Decide which day of the week is best for you to announce the names of the new *Shining Star Students.* Friday morning always worked well for me, because this schedule gave me time during the week to draw the names. The special announcement also becomes something for the students to look forward to at the end of the week. I keep track of how often each child becomes a *Shining Star Student*, so that as many children as possible receive recognition during the year. The average is usually twice a year per child.

WHERE:

After the *Shining Star Students* are introduced on the morning announcements, have them assemble at a central location to receive the certificates and/or a small reward or treat. I usually choose the main office, as most students know where it is and can get to it quickly.

HOW:

Reproduce:

- ☐ *Shining Star Student Nomination* forms (page 12) for each grade level. Color-code the slips by grade level. Example: First-grade slips are red, second-grade slips are blue, etc.). Distribute the forms to the appropriate teachers.

- ☐ *Shining Star Certificate* for each selected student (page 13)

Purchase additional rewards such as pencils with the current *Word Of The Month* or featured character trait printed on them and an edible treat in accordance with your school's food policy.

Record the names of the children recognized on class lists their teachers provide.

Make or buy a *Shining Star Treasure Chest* in which the students deposit their *Shining Star Student Nomination* forms. It should be placed in a central location so students can easily deposit the slips whenever they receive them.

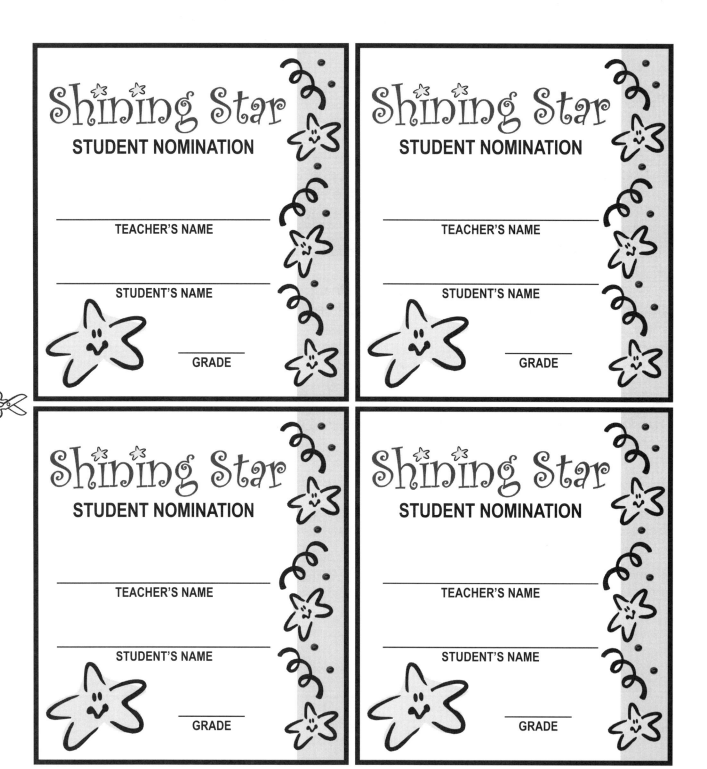

Congratulations!

_____

IS A

Shining Star

AT

_____
SCHOOL NAME

You have been a good role model in
one or more of the following categories:

Caring • Citizenship • Confidence • Cooperation
Courage • Fairness • Honesty • Perseverance
Respect • Responsibility • Tolerance • Work Ethic

_____　　　　　_____
COUNSELOR　　　　　　　　　　DATE

GAME PLAN 2

WHO:

Students in grades K-6

WHAT: SHINING STAR GUIDANCE IN A BAG

The *Shining Star Guidance In A Bag* program involves having specially chosen books and videos/DVDs available for families to sign out and take home to read/view when faced with a conflict or family crisis.

PROGRAM IN ACTION:

An example of this program could be receiving a phone call from a recently divorced parent concerned about behaviors his/her child is exhibiting.

The counselor explains the *Shining Star Guidance In A Bag* program and suggests a special divorce-themed book/video/DVD that can be sent home with the parent's child that afternoon. They can read/watch it together and discuss, in the privacy of their own home, some of the problems the family is experiencing.

After parent and child have this discussion, the counselor schedules a time to meet with the child to talk about divorce-related problems he/she may be having.

WHEN:

Videos, DVDs, and books are available from September through May. The program is a very positive service and can be introduced at Kindergarten Parent Orientation, Open House, Parent Conferences, or in the course of any other school programs at which you have a chance to interact with parents. The books/videos/DVDs can also be used as a "first step" when a parent calls to discuss a family problem. This immediate response can serve as a temporary solution until you have a chance to meet with the child.

WHERE:

A centrally located display case that can be locked is the best place for housing the books/videos/DVDs. This allows parents to see the actual collection when they visit the school. A flyer describing the *Shining Star Guidance In A Bag* program and directions on how to borrow the materials is sent home at the beginning of the year and updated when new selections become available. It familiarizes parents with the program and how it works.

HOW:

Reproduce:

- ☐ *Shining Star Guidance In A Bag* flyer (page 17) to send home with students or have available for parents who visit the school. Prior to reproducing the flyer, fill in the topics and contact information (see sample on page 16).

Display the collection in the location and way you have selected.

Organize a distribution system. Because of the investment involved and the knowledge you can gain from being aware of who is interested in the collection, it is best if you monitor the distribution system yourself. However, a building secretary or librarian can also be helpful.

Buy the materials for the collection. Be sure to preview each book/video/DVD before purchasing it. Most companies have a preview policy for videos/DVDs. Check publishers' websites or search the Internet for book reviews.

Compile a list of materials. In addition to titles, you may want to include copyright date, appropriate age levels, a short description, running time for media, and any special equipment needed for viewing.

Shining Star
Guidance In A Bag

The *Shining Star Guidance In A Bag* program involves having a specially chosen book, video, or DVD available for families to borrow when faced with a conflict or family crisis.

TOPICS CURRENTLY AVAILABLE

A.D.D.	GOOD MANNERS
ANGER	LYING AND DISHONESTY
BULLYING	MAKING MISTAKES IS OK
DECISION MAKING	PERFECTION AND FEAR OF FAILURE
DISRESPECT AND TEASING	POSITIVE HOMEWORK ATTITUDE
DIVORCE	RESPONSIBILITY
DRUG-ABUSE PREVENTION	SELF-ESTEEM
EFFECTIVE DISCIPLINE	SERIOUS ILLNESS
EFFECTIVE STUDY SKILLS	SMART CHOICES
FEARS AND PHOBIAS	STRESS
FRIENDSHIP	WHINING AND COMPLAINING

FOR MORE INFORMATION, PLEASE CONTACT:

Program Coordinator
Name/Elementary Counselor
Telephone Number

Shining Star
Guidance In A Bag

The *Shining Star Guidance In A Bag* program involves having a specially chosen book, video, or DVD available for families to borrow when faced with a conflict or family crisis.

TOPICS CURRENTLY AVAILABLE

FOR MORE INFORMATION, PLEASE CONTACT:

GAME PLAN 3

WHO:

Students in grades K-4

WHAT: SHINING STAR READS

In this program, the counselor reads a book that focuses on the *Word Of The Month* or character trait in 2-5 classes per month.

PROGRAM IN ACTION:

The *Shining Star Reads* program starts in October. Plan to read that month to each class at the grade level you have selected. Send a flyer asking the teachers to suggest times when it would be convenient for you to visit their classrooms. Then send out a schedule so the teachers will know when to expect you. A day or two before your classroom appearance, send a *Shining Star Reads Reminder Slip* to the teacher.

When you arrive in the classroom, have the children sit on the floor in a carpeted story area, if possible. Then read an age-appropriate book that focuses on the *Word Of The Month* or character trait.

WHEN:

If possible, schedule 2-5 classes per month. The number of classes you schedule will be dependent upon your time commitments. A day or two before your classroom appearance, send a *Shining Star Reads Reminder Slip* to the teacher whose classroom you will be visiting.

WHERE:

The program takes place in the classroom. If possible, the children sit on the floor in a carpeted story area.

HOW:

Reproduce:

☐ *Shining Star Convenient Times* flyer for each teacher selected for the month (page 20)

☐ *Shining Star Reads Schedule* for each teacher selected for the month (page 21)

☐ *Shining Star Reads Reminder* slips for teachers of the selected classes (page 22)

Choose age-appropriate books and assign them according to grade level, so as not to overlap and read the same story each year. You may want to use the library as a resource until you have established your own collection. You can find appropriate books by looking through catalogs or on Internet sites and by asking librarians, teachers, and other counselors for suggestions.

Shining Star

CONVENIENT TIMES

Dear _____ ,
　　　　　TEACHER'S NAME

The *Shining Star Reads* program is available for every K-4 classroom. If you choose to participate in the program, I will arrange a mutually convenient time for me to come to your classroom to read a story about the *Word Of The Month* or character trait. If you are interested in having your classroom participate in this program, please complete the sheet below and return it to me by _____.

The most convenient times for my classroom to participate in the *Shining Star Reads* program are:

The most convenient days of the week for my class to participate in the *Shining Star Reads* program are:

Signed _____
　　　　　　　　　　TEACHER

Shining Star

READS SCHEDULE

MONTH				
MON	**TUE**	**WED**	**THU**	**FRI**

Shining Star
READS REMINDER

I will be in your classroom on _____ from _____ to _____ o'clock.

I will be reading a story based on _____,
which is our *Word Of The Month* and a character trait you and your students have been discussing. Please have the children seated before I arrive.

Thanks!

Please contact me if there is a scheduling conflict!

Shining Star
READS REMINDER

I will be in your classroom on _____ from _____ to _____ o'clock.

I will be reading a story based on _____,
which is our *Word Of The Month* and a character trait you and your students have been discussing. Please have the children seated before I arrive.

Thanks!

Please contact me if there is a scheduling conflict!

GAME PLAN 4

WHO:

Students in grades K-6

WHAT: SHINING STAR VIDEO/DVD SERVICE

Select age-appropriate videos or DVDs that highlight the current *Word Of The Month* or selected character trait (see the *Suggested Words Of The Month/Character Traits* list on page 25). Develop a monthly schedule that includes the dates when each teacher has the video.

PROGRAM IN ACTION:

Introduce the program by distributing a *Shining Star Video/DVD Service* flyer to each teacher. At the beginning of each month, give each teacher a *Shining Star Video/DVD Schedule* indicating when his/her class will have that month's video/DVD. When the teacher's date arrives, he/she receives the video/DVD from the previous teacher on the list. Teachers show the video/DVD to their homeroom students at their convenience during the next two or three days, then pass it along to the next teacher on the list.

WHEN:

Begin and end the *Shining Star Video/DVD Service* with the same teachers each month. This simplifies record keeping and makes it easier to search for a specific video/DVD. Each teacher keeps each video/DVD for two or three days every month. After reviewing the video/DVD with their homeroom students, teachers may have informal classroom discussions on the subject matter with the students.

WHERE:

Teachers show the video/DVD in their classrooms during the designated days on the monthly schedule.

HOW:

Reproduce:

☐ *Shining Star Video/DVD Service* flyer for each teacher (page 26)

☐ *Shining Star Video/DVD Schedule* for each teacher (page 27)

Choose age-appropriate videos for each grade level. Since new videos are always being produced and older ones discontinued, it is best to obtain current catalogs.

SUGGESTED WORDS OF THE MONTH/CHARACTER TRAITS

SEPTEMBER
Work Ethic — Apply your best effort and commit to completing tasks. Make positive choices to have a successful school year.

Jan
OCTOBER
Respect — Show regard for yourself, other people, and property. Say nice words and smile! Lend a helping hand.

Sept.
NOVEMBER
Responsibility — Be accountable for your own behavior. Complete all your homework, listen to your teachers, and treat others kindly.

Oct.
DECEMBER
Caring — Help people in need. Listen to your friends and be considerate of others.

Nov.
JANUARY
Fairness — Take turns, share with friends, and be happy for others when they succeed.

FEBRUARY
Honesty — Tell the truth, admit when you are wrong, and trust in other people.

Dec.
MARCH
Confidence — Be happy with who you are, celebrate your talents, and take a risk by trying something new.

April
APRIL
Citizenship — Volunteer at school, protect your neighborhood, and obey the laws in your community.

May
MAY
Cooperation — Work together. Remember that more is accomplished through teamwork and helping others.

Feb.
JUNE
Tolerance — Accept individual differences. Respect the views and beliefs of other people.

JULY
Perseverance — Don't give up! Stick to a task until it is completed.

March
AUGUST
Courage — Do the right thing even when others don't. Follow your conscience rather than the crowd.

Shining Star

Memo: To All Teachers
From: Counselor
Date:
Re: *Shining Star* Video/DVD Service

Each month, I will send you a schedule that will allow you to plan when to show your homeroom students the video featuring our *Word Of The Month*. You will keep the video for two or three days, then pass it along to the next teacher on the list.

Please let me know if any problems or concerns arise.

Shining Star

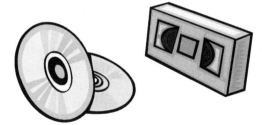

Memo: To All Teachers
From: Counselor
Date:
Re: *Shining Star* Video/DVD Service

Each month, I will send you a schedule that will allow you to plan when to show your homeroom students the video featuring our *Word Of The Month*. You will keep the video for two or three days, then pass it along to the next teacher on the list.

Please let me know if any problems or concerns arise.

Shining Star

VIDEO/DVD SCHEDULE

MON	TUE	WED	THU	FRI
		MONTH		

GAME PLAN 5

WHO:

Students in grades K-2

WHAT: SHINING STAR REWARDS

Each month, teachers are asked to nominate a homeroom student who positively exemplifies the current *Word Of The Month* or selected character trait. When the *Shining Star Fairy* (male: elf or wizard) visits this child's classroom, the child receives a wand (see page 29) and a certificate commending his/her outstanding positive social interaction among his/her peers. The *Shining Star Fairy* is a favorite idea of mine. You may wish to adopt it, use a different presenter, or eliminate the concept altogether.

PROGRAM IN ACTION:

At the beginning of each month, send a *Shining Star Nomination Form* to each teacher of the grade levels involved in the program. Ask the teachers to return the form to you within a week or two. Record the names of the selected students on the *Shining Star Recording Paper*. Double check to make sure that none of the students has received an award earlier in the year, as no student may receive more than one award per year. Complete the *Shining Star Certificates* and arrange them in the order in which you will be visiting classrooms. Include the *Shining Star Fairy* dates on your monthly calendar so the teachers know when to expect you.

Make your classroom visits as elaborate as you wish. If you are using the fairy model, for example, dress in a fairy costume on the designated day before you begin to visit the classrooms. When you enter a classroom, play entrance music and waltz in, tap the chosen child with a wand and present him/her with a *Shining Star Wand* and a certificate. Then tell the whole class how any student can earn a wand the next month. Leave quickly and go on to the next classroom. The whole process should take no more than five minutes per classroom. Teachers like it because it is brief and does not disrupt their schedules.

WHEN:

Each month, each teacher nominates a student who is a positive example of the *Word Of The Month* or selected character trait. Schedule a brief visit to each K-2 class during the last week of the month in order to identify the selected students and make your presentation.

WHERE:

Plan to spend between three and five minutes in each classroom that is to be visited. Visit all the classrooms in one afternoon. If you are not exactly on time, teachers will continue with their afternoon plans until you arrive.

HOW:

Reproduce the following:

- ☐ *Shining Star Nomination Forms* for each teacher (page 30)

- ☐ *Shining Star Recording Papers* for the counselor's records—make copies to record each participating teacher's student selections (page 31)

- ☐ *Shining Star Certificates* for each selected student (page 32)

Purchase inexpensive wands (order from the Oriental Trading Co., www.orientaltrading.com, item numbers: IN-25/210 or IN-25/211) or make a wand for yourself and one for each selected student.

Star Wands:

Materials required for each wand: 4"-5" square piece of disposable plastic, star-shaped pattern, 12" wooden dowel, silver or gold glitter, white craft glue, 12" pieces of ribbon

1. Using a star pattern, cut two stars from the plastic.

2. Coat the edges and one side of the star with white craft glue. Sprinkle the glue with glitter. Allow this to dry completely, then repeat the process on the other star.

3. Glue the two stars together, leaving an opening to insert the wooden dowel.

4. Insert the wooden dowel into the star, then glue the opening to secure the dowel.

5. Tie the ribbons around the base of the star where the dowel has been inserted. Add a touch of glue to keep the ribbon securely in place.

If you are dressing as a fairy, you will need to acquire wings (many stores carry them around Halloween) and a container so you can easily carry the wands from room to room. You may also want to tape entrance music.

Shining Star

NOMINATION FORM

Nominate one homeroom student whom you feel is a true *Shining Star*. The student should exemplify our current *Word Of The Month*.

WORD OF THE MONTH

The student will receive a *Shining Star Wand* on the afternoon of _____ .

If you have any questions, please see _____ .

TEACHER

I nominate _____ to receive a *Shining Star Wand* based on his/her acts of _____ shown to other students and teachers.

Please return nomination form to _____ by _____ .

Thanks!

Shining Star

RECORDING PAPER

Teacher _____   Grade _____

STUDENT CHOSEN FOR THE MONTH OF:

September _____

October _____

November _____

December _____

January _____

February _____

March _____

April _____

May _____

June _____

July _____

August _____

GAME PLAN 6

WHO:

Students in grades K-6

WHAT: SHINING STAR CHECKUPS

Use *Shining Star Checkup Slips* to let your students know you are thinking of them. They are especially effective with students you may have worked with closely and with whom you lost contact after their problem was resolved.

PROGRAM IN ACTION:

Reproduce a large number of *Shining Star Checkup Slips* at the beginning of the program so you will have an ample supply on hand. At the beginning of each month, review the past month's student referrals and decide which students you might like to check in with.

WHEN:

Leave *Shining Star Checkup Slips* on the students' desks before the school day begins. Some students will respond by sending you a note. But whether they respond or not, the students will know you were thinking about them.

WHERE:

Leave the notes on the students' desks or give them to the teachers to distribute.

HOW:

Reproduce the following:

☐ *Shining Star Checkup Slips* to distribute to students throughout the year (pages 34-38)

Shining Star

You are listening to your teacher and completing your work!

Bravo!

From:

I heard that your grades are improving and that you are doing your homework!

Great Job!

From: _____ Shining Star

You are a **Great Kid!**
I am glad I know you!

From: _____

Shining Star

Just thinking about you
and hoping everything is OK.

Let me know if you need to talk.

Drop me a note sometime.

Shining Star

From: _____

I heard you have been doing a

Great Job

in class.

Keep up the good work!

From: _____

I heard you have been doing a

Great Job

in class.

Keep up the good work!

From: _____

I know you have a lot going on at home right now.

Let me know if you need to talk about anything.

From: _____

Shining Star

Yes I need to talk about: _____
_____
_____
_____ .

No I am OK right now, but I will let you know if I need to talk later.

Your Name: _____

(Please put in my mailbox.)

GAME PLAN 7

WHO:

Students in grades K-3

WHAT: SHINING STAR COLORING CONTEST

Once a month, distribute a coloring sheet depicting your school's *Word Of The Month* or a character trait of your choice. The students may color these sheets at school or at home. They turn them in to their teachers, who place them in your mailbox by the 15th of every month. You then select as many winners as you like. You could choose one winner per grade level, one per class, or whatever number would best reflect the school's interests. Winners are selected on the basis of neatness, or being the most colorful, most creative, or the counselor's choice. Winners' names are announced over the school's public address system. Each winner receives a certificate and a small reward such as a special pencil, pen or crayons, pencil sharpener, eraser, etc. The winning pictures are displayed for the remainder of the month.

PROGRAM IN ACTION:

Select the coloring sheet for the month. There are 12 coloring sheets included in this program, one for each *Word Of The Month* (page 25). If any of these character traits are not traits your school is emphasizing, cross out the title at the top of the page and replace it with a trait your students are studying. Reproduce the number of coloring sheets required for the month and distribute them to the students. Tell the students to complete the coloring sheet, either at school or at home, by the required date and return the completed sheet to their teachers. The teachers will put the completed coloring sheets in the counselor's mailbox. Within a few days, the counselor chooses the winners and introduces them on the morning announcements. The winning students come to the office for their certificates and prizes. The counselor then displays the winning pictures for all to see. (*Note*: Keep track of the winners. Students may win only once a year.)

WHEN:

Visit each classroom on the first day of the month in which you begin the program. Explain the program to the students, show them the first coloring sheet, and distribute one coloring sheet to each student. After the initial visit, distribute new coloring sheets to the homeroom teachers on the first of each month. Collect the completed coloring sheets on the 15th of the month and announce the winners as soon after that as possible.

WHERE:

The students may color the sheets at home or at school. The winners are announced on the morning announcements, and the rewards are given out as the students come to the office. Winning pictures are displayed in a central location to support the *Word Of The Month* program or other character-education programs.

HOW:

Reproduce the following:

☐ *Word Of The Month* coloring sheet for each student (pages 41-52)

☐ *Word Of The Month Coloring Contest Winner* certificate for each winning student (pages 53-56)

Purchase small rewards for coloring-contest winners.

WORK ETHIC

NAME: _____

TEACHER: _____

Monthly *Shining Star* Coloring Contest
Entries must be returned to the counselor by the 15th of each month to be eligible for prizes. Color the picture featuring the *Word Of The Month* as carefully and creatively as you can. Winners will be announced on the morning announcements. Your picture will be judged for neatness, creativity, and colorfulness. Have fun!

RESPECT

NAME: _____

TEACHER: _____

Monthly *Shining Star* Coloring Contest
Entries must be returned to the counselor by the 15th of each month to be eligible for prizes. Color the picture featuring the *Word Of The Month* as carefully and creatively as you can. Winners will be announced on the morning announcements. Your picture will be judged for neatness, creativity, and colorfulness. Have fun!

RESPONSIBILITY

NAME: _____

TEACHER: _____

Monthly *Shining Star* Coloring Contest
Entries must be returned to the counselor by the 15th of each month to be eligible for prizes. Color the picture featuring the *Word Of The Month* as carefully and creatively as you can. Winners will be announced on the morning announcements. Your picture will be judged for neatness, creativity, and colorfulness. Have fun!

CARING

NAME: _____

TEACHER: _____

Monthly *Shining Star* Coloring Contest
Entries must be returned to the counselor by the 15th of each month to be eligible for prizes. Color the picture featuring the *Word Of The Month* as carefully and creatively as you can. Winners will be announced on the morning announcements. Your picture will be judged for neatness, creativity, and colorfulness. Have fun!

FAIRNESS

NAME: _____

TEACHER: _____

Monthly *Shining Star* Coloring Contest

Entries must be returned to the counselor by the 15th of each month to be eligible for prizes. Color the picture featuring the *Word Of The Month* as carefully and creatively as you can. Winners will be announced on the morning announcements. Your picture will be judged for neatness, creativity, and colorfulness. Have fun!

HONESTY

NAME: _____

TEACHER: _____

Monthly *Shining Star* Coloring Contest
Entries must be returned to the counselor by the 15th of each month to be eligible for prizes. Color the picture featuring the *Word Of The Month* as carefully and creatively as you can. Winners will be announced on the morning announcements. Your picture will be judged for neatness, creativity, and colorfulness. Have fun!

CONFIDENCE

NAME: _____

TEACHER: _____

Shining Star

Monthly *Shining Star* Coloring Contest
Entries must be returned to the counselor by the 15th of each month to be eligible for prizes. Color the picture featuring the *Word Of The Month* as carefully and creatively as you can. Winners will be announced on the morning announcements. Your picture will be judged for neatness, creativity, and colorfulness. Have fun!

CITIZENSHIP

NAME: _____

TEACHER: _____

Monthly *Shining Star* Coloring Contest
Entries must be returned to the counselor by the 15th of each month to be eligible for prizes. Color the picture featuring the *Word Of The Month* as carefully and creatively as you can. Winners will be announced on the morning announcements. Your picture will be judged for neatness, creativity, and colorfulness. Have fun!

COOPERATION

NAME: _____

TEACHER: _____

Monthly *Shining Star* Coloring Contest
Entries must be returned to the counselor by the 15th of each month to be eligible for prizes. Color the picture featuring the *Word Of The Month* as carefully and creatively as you can. Winners will be announced on the morning announcements. Your picture will be judged for neatness, creativity, and colorfulness. Have fun!

TOLERANCE

NAME: _____

TEACHER: _____

Monthly *Shining Star* Coloring Contest
Entries must be returned to the counselor by the 15th of each month to be eligible for prizes. Color the picture featuring the *Word Of The Month* as carefully and creatively as you can. Winners will be announced on the morning announcements. Your picture will be judged for neatness, creativity, and colorfulness. Have fun!

PERSEVERANCE

NAME: _____

TEACHER: _____

Monthly *Shining Star* Coloring Contest

Entries must be returned to the counselor by the 15th of each month to be eligible for prizes. Color the picture featuring the *Word Of The Month* as carefully and creatively as you can. Winners will be announced on the morning announcements. Your picture will be judged for neatness, creativity, and colorfulness. Have fun!

Shining Star

COURAGE

NAME: _____

TEACHER: _____

Shining Star

Monthly *Shining Star* Coloring Contest
Entries must be returned to the counselor by the 15th of each month to be eligible for prizes. Color the picture featuring the *Word Of The Month* as carefully and creatively as you can. Winners will be announced on the morning announcements. Your picture will be judged for neatness, creativity, and colorfulness. Have fun!

CONGRATULATIONS!

_____

is a

Shining Star

Word Of The Month
Coloring-Contest Winner

CATEGORY:

Neatness

From: _____

GAME PLAN 8

WHO:

Students in grades 4-6

WHAT: SHINING STAR POSTER CONTEST

Each month, distribute a poster contest sheet featuring your school's *Word Of The Month* or a character trait of your choice with a definition of the word attached. (See page 25 for *Suggested Words Of The Month/Character Traits* and definitions.) The students then design a poster to portray the selected word. This can be done either at school or at home. The students turn their posters in to their teachers, who place them in the counselor's mailbox by the 15th of every month. The counselor selects the number of winners there will be. You could select one per grade level, one per class, or whatever number would best reflect the school's interests. Selections are based on neatness, colorfulness, creativity, and the counselor's choice. Winners' names are announced over the school's public address system. Each winner receives a certificate and a small reward such as a special pencil, pen or crayons, pencil sharpener, eraser, etc. The winning pictures are displayed for the remainder of the month.

PROGRAM IN ACTION:

Reproduce one poster sheet and write the selected character trait on the blank line. Then, using that poster sheet, reproduce the number of poster sheets required for the month. Distribute them to the students, telling them to complete the poster, either at school or at home, by the required date and return the completed posters to their teachers. The teachers will put the completed posters in the counselor's mailbox. Within a few days, you choose the winners and introduce them on the morning announcements. The winning students come to the office to receive their certificates and prizes. Display the winning pictures for everyone to see. (*Note*: Keep track of the winners, as students may win only once a year.)

WHEN:

Visit each classroom on the first day of the month in which you begin the program. Explain the program to the students, show them the first poster sheet, and distribute one poster sheet to each student. After the initial visit, distribute new coloring sheets to the homeroom teachers on the first of each month. Collect the completed coloring sheets on the 15th of the month and announce the winners as soon after that as possible.

WHERE:

The students may design their posters at home or at school. The winners are introduced on the morning announcements, and the rewards are distributed when the students come to the office. Winning pictures are displayed in a central location to support the *Word Of The Month* or another character-education program.

HOW:

Reproduce the following:

☐ *Shining Star Poster Contest* sheet for each student (page 59)

☐ *Shining Star Character Trait Of The Month Poster Winner* for each winner (page 60)

Purchase small rewards for coloring-contest winners.

Shining Star Poster Contest

_____

NAME: _____ **TEACHER:** _____

Entries are due by the 15th of each month to be eligible for prizes.

GAME PLAN 9

WHO:

Students in grades K-6

WHAT: DINE-AND-DISCUSS LUNCHEONS

The *Dine-And-Discuss Luncheons* program encourages parents to become aware of responsibility, organizational skills, study habits, and other skills their children may be striving to develop.

PROGRAM IN ACTION:

On the day of the luncheon, the parents spend approximately 20 minutes eating lunch with their children. The other 20-30 minutes of the lunch period is devoted to an educational activity. Since parents and children participate in the activity together, it must be something that both can relate to and enjoy. Educational bingo games work very well (see suggestions on page 62). After the children return to their classrooms, ask the parents to complete the *Dine-And-Discuss Luncheon Evaluation* before leaving.

WHEN:

Each month, invite one teacher's class to participate in the *Dine-And-Discuss Luncheon*. Reproduce the invitations. (See the sample invitation on page 63. Use it as a guide to complete parents' invitation on page 64). Then visit the designated class, talk about the luncheon, and distribute the invitations to the students to take home. Ask the classroom teacher to record the R.S.V.P.s.

WHERE:

The luncheon takes place during the classroom teacher's regularly scheduled lunch period. The invitation specifies the time and asks parents to bring a brown-bag or fast-food lunch for themselves and their child.

HOW:

Reproduce the following:

- ☐ An adapted *Dine-And-Discuss Luncheon* parents' invitation for each student (page 64)
- ☐ *Dine-And-Discuss Luncheon Evaluation* for each parent (page 65)

SUGGESTED BINGO GAMES
Published by Mar*co Products, Inc.

Responsibility Bingo Focuses on responsibility for self, home, friends, school, and the world
Grades 2-5

Respect Bingo Focuses on caring for self, working with others, responsibility at home, fairness in play, and trustworthy actions
Grades 2-5

Friendship Bingo Focuses on things associated with friendship: feelings, character traits, behaviors, pitfalls, and how to begin a friendship
Grades 2-5

Manners Bingo Focuses on learning good manners while developing thinking skills
Grades 3-8

Stress-Less Bingo Focuses on managing stress about school, at home, self, time, and the world
Grades 2-5

Feelings Bingo Focuses on helping students understand both their own feelings and those of others
Grades K-5

SAMPLE INVITATION

SCHOOL NAME/LOGO

Dear Parents or Guardians:

You and your _____-grade son or daughter in (TEACHER'S NAME) class are cordially invited to join (COUNSELOR'S NAME) on (DAY AND DATE) for an informal lunchtime get-together. Please bring a fast-food or brown-bag lunch for yourself and your child to enjoy. Your child will not be allowed to buy lunch at school that day. We will dine from (TIME) in the (PLACE), then enjoy a fun activity from (TIME). Please call me at (PHONE #) if you have any questions concerning the luncheon.

I hope you will be able to take a break from your busy schedule and dine with your child. The topic of the day will be (RESPONSIBILITY.)

Please return the response form below to your child's homeroom teacher by (DATE) to R.S.V.P. for the luncheon.

Thank you,

(COUNSELOR'S SIGNATURE)

✂ ─────────────────────────────────────

Your name _____

Child's name _____

☐ **YES**, I will be attending the *Dine-And-Discuss Luncheon*.

(I have room to accommodate the first 15 parents who respond and their children.)

63

SCHOOL-WIDE GUIDANCE: BE A SHINING STAR! © 2007 MAR*CO PRODUCTS, INC. 1-800-448-2197

Dear Parents or Guardians:

You and your ____-grade son or daughter in _____ class are cordially invited to join _____ on _____ for an informal lunchtime get-together. Please bring a fast-food or brown-bag lunch for yourself and your child to enjoy. Your child will not be allowed to buy lunch at school that day. We will dine from _____ in the _____ , then enjoy a fun activity from _____ . Please call me at _____ if you have any questions concerning the luncheon.

I hope you will be able to take a break from your busy schedule and dine with your child. The topic of the day will be_____ .

Please return the response form below to your child's homeroom teacher by _____ to R.S.V.P. for the luncheon.

Thank you,

✂ -

Your name_____

Child's name_____

☐ **YES**, I will be attending the *Dine-And-Discuss Luncheon*.

(I have room to accommodate the first _____ parents who respond and their children.)

Evaluation

MY NAME _____

MY CHILD'S NAME _____

Please give your opinion of our program.

1. The program was fun, educational, and interesting. 1 = Poor 10 = Exceptional.

    1···2···3···4···5···6···7···8···9···10

2. I liked _____ the best.

3. One thing that could be improved is _____
   _____
   _____

4. Would you attend another *Dine-And-Discuss Luncheon?*

    ☐ Yes   ☐ No

    If yes, what would you like the topic to be? _____

 Thank you,

GAME PLAN 10

WHO:

Students in grades K-6

WHAT: WORD OF THE MONTH OR CHARACTER TRAIT GROUPS

PROGRAM IN ACTION:

Teachers may find that classroom students exhibit behaviors that show that they do not understand the meaning of the character trait or *Word Of The Month* being emphasized. For these students, a small-group meeting focusing on the trait is effective. A *Referral Form* will be available each month so teachers may nominate a student in their class to join other students from the same or adjoining grade levels for this small-group meeting. After the group meeting, a letter describing it is sent to each parent.

WHEN:

The students meet only once, unless their teachers refer them to other groups during the year. Schedule the meeting at a time that is convenient for both the counselor and the teacher.

WHERE:

Meet with small groups of 4-5 students in the guidance office or another convenient small room.

HOW:

Choose a game or activity that will complement the character trait or *Word Of The Month* being emphasized. (A list of appropriate games is found on page 67.)

Reproduce the following:

- ☐ *Referral Form* to send to teachers (page 68). Reproduce one form, fill in the topic of the month, then reproduce enough forms for the teachers.

- ☐ *Notification Form* that is sent to parents after the group meeting (page 69)

Set up a small-group schedule and notify the teachers of it.

SUGGESTED GAMES
Published by Mar*co Products, Inc.

Caring	Catch A Friend Game (Grades 1-3)
Citizenship	School Rules Game (Grades 1-5) Character Dominoes (Grades 2-5)
Confidence	Dream, Think, Image! Game (Grades 1-5) Answer Me Game (Grades 3-5)
Cooperation	Social Safari Game (Grades 3-5) Focus On Friendship Game (Grades 2-5)
Courage	Bully Buster Bingo (Grades 2-7) Bully Proof Bingo (Grades (K-2)
Fairness	Kids Count Game (Grades 2-5)
Honesty	Character Dominoes (Grades 2-5)
Perseverance	Escape From Loneliness Island Game (Grades 1-5)
Respect	Keep Your Cool Game (Grades 3-6) Mighty Angry Dude Game (Grades 2-5)
Responsibility	The Responsibility Game (Grades 1-5)
Tolerance	Multicultural Bingo (Grades 1-6)
Work Ethic	School Rules Game (Grades 1-5)

Shining Star Guidance Program

REFERRAL FORM

TOPIC _____

TEACHER'S NAME _____

STUDENT'S NAME _____

Guidelines for referral: A child may be referred for this type of intervention once a year.

Please return this form by _____
if you would like one of your students to be placed in a small group to facilitate understanding of the topic above. This is a one-time meeting.

SCHEDULE

(This schedule will be returned to notify you of the time and date the group will meet.)

Date _____

Time: _____

Dear _____-Grade Parent/Guardian,

Today your child met with _____, the counselor, and several other _____-grade students to discuss _____, the character trait the students are studying this month. We played a game, read a book, or participated in an activity to help your child gain a better understanding of how to apply our topic here at _____School.

These groups meet once a month, with different students selected to participate each month. Your child was selected this month! Please contact me if you have any questions or concerns. Thank you.

_____
COUNSELOR

_____
TELEPHONE NUMBER

Shining Star Guidance Program

Shining Star

MONTHLY SCHOOL-WIDE GUIDANCE PROGRAMS

GAME PLAN 1 FOR SCHOOL-WIDE GUIDANCE
(SEPTEMBER)

WHO:

Kindergarten students

WHAT: HOW TO HAVE A SUCCESSFUL SCHOOL YEAR FOR YOU AND YOUR CHILD

A workshop for Kindergarten parents

PROGRAM IN ACTION:

Parents love to get involved and learn some of the ins and outs of their child's first school experience. Send home the *How To Have A Successful School Year For You And Your Child* flyer a few days before the program is scheduled to take place.

Before the parents arrive on the day of the workshop, tape the *Headers* to the wall around the room. Tape five *Point Value Cards* (10, 20, 30, 40, and 50) below each *Header*.

Food is a great icebreaker. Coffee and tea, juice, and doughnuts are usually a good choice to set out and serve when the parents arrive. Begin with a short question-and-answer period, then move into the *How Well Do You Know (<u>THE NAME OF YOUR SCHOOL</u>) School? Game*. The game takes about 30 minutes and addresses many of the parents' concerns or questions. The parents earn points, and it is fun to have a few prizes for the winners. Conclude the workshop with another question-and-answer period or a quick tour of the school.

WHEN:

The workshop takes place on one of the mornings of the first full week of school. (An alternate plan would be to hold the workshop on a Parent/Teacher Conference Night in the fall and include all grade levels.)

WHERE:

Hold the workshop in a spare classroom or in the school cafeteria. The room must accommodate 25-30 persons and be available for approximately one hour.

HOW:

Reproduce the following:

- ☐ *How To Have A Successful School Year For You And Your Child* flyer for each kindergarten student (page 74)

- ☐ *How Well Do You Know _____ School? Game* directions for play (page 75)

- ☐ *Point Value Cards* for each *Header* (page 76)

- ☐ *Game Headers* (pages 77-82)

- ☐ *How Well Do You Know _____ School? Game* questions and answers (pages 83-85)

Cut apart the *Point Value Cards*.

Using masking tape, tape the *Headers* to the wall around the room. Tape five *Point Value Cards* (10, 20, 30, 40, and 50) below each *Header*.

Purchase food such as coffee, tea, juice, and doughnuts to serve parents.

Purchase prizes for parents, such as small parenting books or books that can be read to their child.

Do you want your child to do his/her best in school?
Do you want your child to have that "I CAN DO IT" feeling?
Do you want your child to become more responsible?

LEARN HOW YOU
CAN HELP YOUR CHILD
BY ATTENDING THE

HOW TO HAVE A SUCCESSFUL SCHOOL YEAR FOR YOU AND YOUR CHILD

WORKSHOP FOR PARENTS

PLACE: _____

DATE: _____

TIME: _____

GIVEN BY: _____

FOR RESERVATIONS, PLEASE CALL:

(_____) _____

OR

(_____) _____

Shining Star Guidance Program

HOW WELL DO YOU KNOW _____ SCHOOL? GAME

DIRECTIONS FOR PLAY:

Tape the *Headers* horizontally on a large chalkboard or wall. Then tape five point values under each category. Start with 10 and continue on through 50. You are now set to play the game.

Begin by having one parent choose a category and point value. Using the *Question-And-Answers* sheet, read the question to the parent. If he/she answers correctly, have him/her take the *Point Value Card* from the wall and keep it until the end of the game. If the parent answers the question incorrectly, move to the person directly to his/her left and continue moving in that direction until someone answers the question correctly.

Go to the person directly to the left of the parent who started the game and have that person choose a category and point value. Continue the game in this manner until all of the questions have been answered. Have the parents add up their *Point Value Cards.* Award prizes to those with the most points.

POINT VALUE CARDS

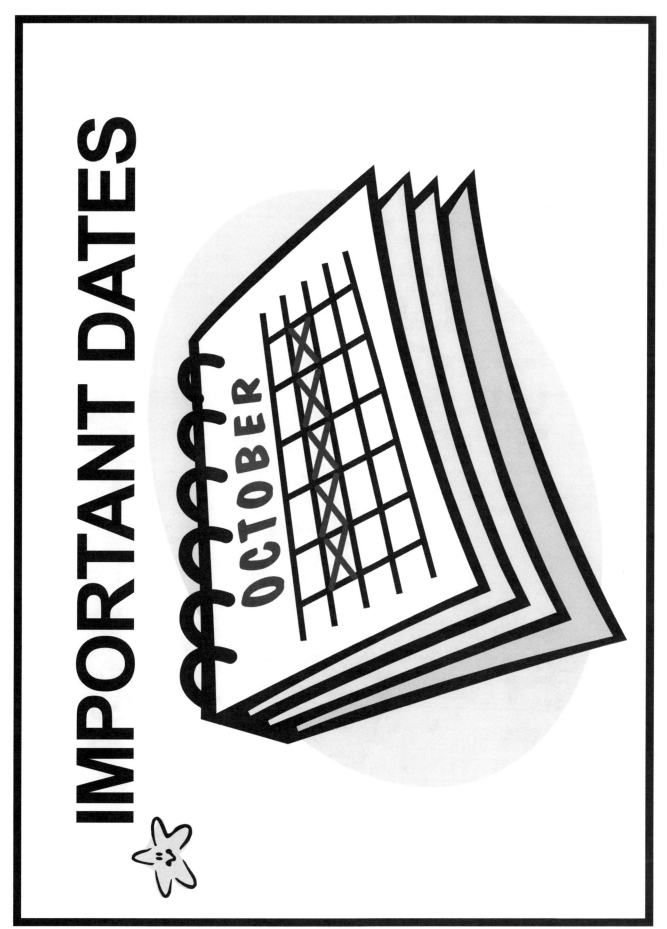

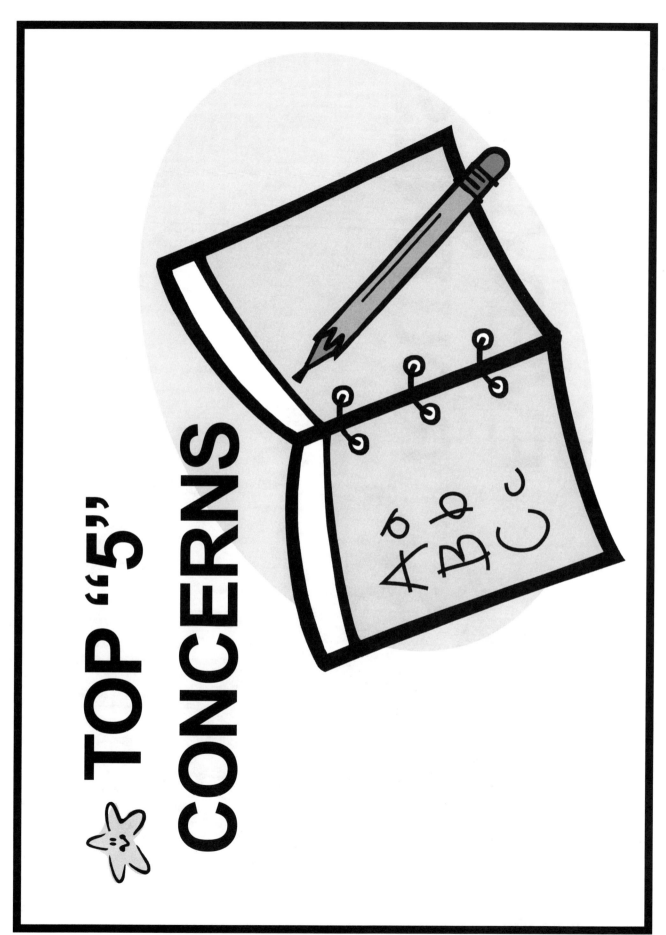

IMPORTANT PEOPLE IN OUR SCHOOL

VOLUNTEERING OPPORTUNITIES

HOW WELL DO YOU KNOW _____ SCHOOL? GAME

QUESTIONS AND ANSWERS

Important Dates

(For this category, select five important dates that parents should know about. Assign each a point value. You may choose Parent/Teacher Conference Days, holiday breaks, teacher in-service days, or anything else that is special, such as a Book Fair.)

10 _____

20 _____

30 _____

40 _____

50 _____

Helpful Habits

10 What helpful habit do you teach children when you set a regular time to pick up playthings? (to put things away)

20 What helpful habit do children learn when you put them to bed early each night and get them up at the same time each morning? (to follow a schedule)

30 What helpful habit do you teach children when you make them responsible for taking out the trash, setting the table, etc.? (to participate in simple household chores)

40 What helpful habit do children learn when they have the ability to work with others plus a sense of caring and sharing? (to get along with others)

50 What helpful habit do children acquire when they follow directions, which is a necessity at school? (to listen)

Important People In Our School

10 Who is the person who visits the school (<u>NUMBER OF DAYS</u>) each week, administers medicine, and calls parents if their child is ill? (nurse)

20 Who is the person you must call when your child is sick and not coming to school on a specific day? (secretary)

30 Who is the person you might contact if your child is experiencing unusual fears about school or a family problem? (guidance counselor)

40 Who is the person to contact if your child is experiencing behavior problems at school or you have a concern that you and your child's teacher cannot work out? (principal)

50 Who is the person to contact when you are upset by your child's academic progress or have a classroom concern? (teacher)

Top "5" Concerns

10 What is it called when a child cries when Mom or Dad leaves him or her at school? (separation anxiety)

20 What is it called when children hit or call other children names in order to intimidate them? (bullying)

30 What is it called when children get lower and lower grades in class, do not want to try to learn a new skill, or use a negative behavior to get out of class? (academic failure)

40 What is it called when a child tells a teacher something unimportant solely for the purpose of getting another child into trouble? (tattling)

50 What might be the next step when a child is just not picking up things fast enough and seems to have an attention span of no more than 30 seconds? (individual testing)

Everyday Routines

10   To make sure you see and know about everything your child brings home, what should you do every night? (check your child's backpack)

20   What should you do to all personal belongings your child brings to school? (write your child's name on them with a permanent marker)

30   What is it called when you pick out the clothes to be worn the next day, make sure your child is asleep before 9 p.m., get your child up on time each day, have him or her eat a good breakfast, etc.? (following a schedule)

40   What usually takes about 20 minutes each night? (homework)

50   What is it called when each day your child tells you about what happened in school? (listening)

Volunteering Opportunities

10   What is the organization that moms and dads can join to help out with school activities? (PTA)

20   Who is the person who helps at holiday parties by providing games and activities? (room parent)

30   Who is the person who accompanies your child's class on field trips to places like the zoo? (field trip chaperone)

40   Who is the person who helps out in your child's classroom once a week by laminating materials, sorting items, and doing other tasks the classroom teacher requests? (classroom volunteer)

50   Who is the person who volunteers to help a child with reading skills? (<u>NAME OF THE PROGRAM USED IN YOUR SCHOOL</u> volunteer)

GAME PLAN 2 FOR SCHOOL-WIDE GUIDANCE (OCTOBER)

WHO:

Students in grades K-6

WHAT: RED RIBBON WEEK

PROGRAM IN ACTION:

Red Ribbon Week is a celebration of the drug-free lifestyle. Students enjoy participating in spirit activities each day throughout the week and this helps raise their awareness that they can choose not to use drugs.

It is important to have all *Red Ribbon Week* materials and handouts organized a week in advance. Send home *Red Ribbon Week* flyers the Friday before *Red Ribbon Week* begins. Make teachers aware of the activities through the *Red Ribbon Week Teachers' Instructions*. If you serve several schools, it is wise to have a designated teacher or secretary pass out the stickers or items each day during *Red Ribbon Week*. If you have the items ready to distribute, they are usually happy to help.

On the day of the activities, distribute the appropriate items and watch the students enjoy the spirit of the drug-free message being sent.

WHEN:

Red Ribbon Week is the third or fourth week in October each year.

WHERE:

All classroom activities can be easily conducted with teacher assistance.

HOW:

Reproduce the following:

- ☐ *Red Ribbon Week* flyer for each student (page 87)
- ☐ *Red Ribbon Week Teachers' Instructions* for each teacher (page 88)
- ☐ *"Hug Not Drugs" Day* coupons for each student (page 89)

Purchase small incentive items such as stickers, candy, etc.

RED RIBBON WEEK

_____
(INSERT DATE)

Please show your support for a drug-free lifestyle by wearing appropriate clothing on these special days.

Monday: *Good Character, Good Choice!*
Wear RED clothing

Tuesday: *Show Your "Drug-Free" School Spirit*
Wear SCHOOL COLORS

Wednesday: *Living a Drug-Free Lifestyle is "No Sweat"*
Wear "SWEAT" pants, jackets, shirts, etc.

Thursday: *"Hugs Not Drugs"*
Bring your favorite STUFFED ANIMAL to school

Students wearing their red ribbons to school today will receive a coupon to place in a drawing for a *Red Ribbon Week* prize!

Friday: *"Drugs Are Batty"*
Wear ORANGE and BLACK

Sponsored by your "Safe and Drug-Free Schools" Committee

RED RIBBON WEEK

_____
(INSERT DATE)

TEACHERS' INSTRUCTIONS*

Please show your support for a drug-free lifestyle by wearing appropriate clothing on these special days.

Monday: ***Good Character, Good Choice!***
Wear RED clothing
*Give out *Red Ribbons*

Tuesday: ***Show Your "Drug-Free" School Spirit***
Wear SCHOOL COLORS
*Give each student an anti-drug sticker

Wednesday: ***Living a Drug-Free Lifestyle is "No Sweat"***
Wear "SWEAT" pants, jackets, shirts, etc.
*Give out *Red Ribbon Week* lollipops

Thursday: ***"Hugs Not Drugs"***
Bring your favorite STUFFED ANIMAL to school
*Give out coupons to students still wearing their *Red Ribbons*. Students may write their names on the coupons and put them in a box in the guidance office to enter a drawing to win a *Red Ribbon Week* prize!

Friday: ***"Drugs Are Batty"***
Wear ORANGE and BLACK
*Give each student an anti-drug sticker

Sponsored by your "Safe and Drug-Free Schools" Committee

GAME PLAN 3 FOR SCHOOL-WIDE GUIDANCE (NOVEMBER)

WHO:

Students in grades K-6

WHAT: BYE, BYE, BULLIES

PROGRAM IN ACTION:

It is very helpful to offer a guidance activity during Parent/Teacher Conferences. *Bye, Bye, Bullies* concentrates on positive responses that students and parents can use when confronted by a bully. You can buy an inexpensive lollipop tree (one source is the Oriental Trading Co., www.orientaltrading.com) and mark the bottoms of the lollipops with different-colored markers. When a student picks a lollipop off a tree, he or she must answer a *Bye, Bye, Bully Situation Card* drawn from a container. Whether the student gets the answer right or wrong, this provides a valuable teaching moment. The student gets to keep the lollipop and, depending upon the color of the bottom of the lollipop, may qualify for a prize. Examples of prizes would be: stress-reduction balls, *Word Of The Month* pencils, prizes with your school's name on them, stickers, etc.

This short interactive guidance session is very valuable in establishing the counselor as a school friend who can help in times of need.

WHEN:

Plan the activity during Parent/Teacher Conferences at your school. One of two days before the conferences, send home flyers alerting the parents to your activity.

WHERE:

Set up your activity in a place that students and parents pass on their way to or from conferences. This could be in a hallway, the guidance office, the main office, or any other convenient space.

HOW:

Reproduce the following:

- ☐ *Bye, Bye, Bully Situation Cards* (pages 92-93)
- ☐ *Bye, Bye, Bully Invitation* flyer for each student (page 94)

Purchase the following:

- ☐ A lollipop tree (You could also use a jar or bucket and have the students reach in and pick a lollipop or another edible treat in accordance with your school's food policy.)
- ☐ Lollipops
- ☐ Prizes to be given away

Your friend has a club and says that another student cannot be in the club because she does not have blonde hair. *What would you say or do?* *BYE, BYE, BULLY SITUATION CARD* *SCHOOL-WIDE CLASSROOM GUIDANCE* © 2007 MAR•CO PRODUCTS, INC. 1-800-448-2197	A student threatens to beat you up during lunch. *What should you do?* *BYE, BYE, BULLY SITUATION CARD* *SCHOOL-WIDE CLASSROOM GUIDANCE* © 2007 MAR•CO PRODUCTS, INC. 1-800-448-2197
Several kids are making fun of a student's new haircut. *What could you say or do to help him/her feel better?* *BYE, BYE, BULLY SITUATION CARD* *SCHOOL-WIDE CLASSROOM GUIDANCE* © 2007 MAR•CO PRODUCTS, INC. 1-800-448-2197	One of the students in your class always sticks his/her foot out and trips you when you go to the science table. *What can you do?* *BYE, BYE, BULLY SITUATION CARD* *SCHOOL-WIDE CLASSROOM GUIDANCE* © 2007 MAR•CO PRODUCTS, INC. 1-800-448-2197
A student calls you "Stupid." *What would you say or do?* *BYE, BYE, BULLY SITUATION CARD* *SCHOOL-WIDE CLASSROOM GUIDANCE* © 2007 MAR•CO PRODUCTS, INC. 1-800-448-2197	Your good friend says that you can't sit with him/her at lunch today. *What would you do or say?* *BYE, BYE, BULLY SITUATION CARD* *SCHOOL-WIDE CLASSROOM GUIDANCE* © 2007 MAR•CO PRODUCTS, INC. 1-800-448-2197
You are pushed off the swings. *What should you do?* *BYE, BYE, BULLY SITUATION CARD* *SCHOOL-WIDE CLASSROOM GUIDANCE* © 2007 MAR•CO PRODUCTS, INC. 1-800-448-2197	You notice that one of your class-mates does not have anyone to play with at recess. *How could you help to make the situation better?* *BYE, BYE, BULLY SITUATION CARD* *SCHOOL-WIDE CLASSROOM GUIDANCE* © 2007 MAR•CO PRODUCTS, INC. 1-800-448-2197
Everyone always makes fun of a student in your class because he/she never gives the right answer. *How could you help the situation?* *BYE, BYE, BULLY SITUATION CARD* *SCHOOL-WIDE CLASSROOM GUIDANCE* © 2007 MAR•CO PRODUCTS, INC. 1-800-448-2197	A student keeps kicking you on the bus. *What can you do or say?* *BYE, BYE, BULLY SITUATION CARD* *SCHOOL-WIDE CLASSROOM GUIDANCE* © 2007 MAR•CO PRODUCTS, INC. 1-800-448-2197

Your friend says that you cannot play with him/her today. *What would you do or say?* BYE, BYE, BULLY SITUATION CARD *SCHOOL-WIDE CLASSROOM GUIDANCE* © 2007 MAR*CO PRODUCTS, INC. 1-800-448-2197	A student makes fun of your brother/sister and calls him/her names. *What can you do or say?* BYE, BYE, BULLY SITUATION CARD *SCHOOL-WIDE CLASSROOM GUIDANCE* © 2007 MAR*CO PRODUCTS, INC. 1-800-448-2197
A student drops his/her books all over the floor. Everyone is laughing at him/her. *What can you do or say?* BYE, BYE, BULLY SITUATION CARD *SCHOOL-WIDE CLASSROOM GUIDANCE* © 2007 MAR*CO PRODUCTS, INC. 1-800-448-2197	Your friend always offers to let you cut into the lunch line. *What can you do or say?* BYE, BYE, BULLY SITUATION CARD *SCHOOL-WIDE CLASSROOM GUIDANCE* © 2007 MAR*CO PRODUCTS, INC. 1-800-448-2197
A classmate calls your best friend "fat." *What would you do or say?* BYE, BYE, BULLY SITUATION CARD *SCHOOL-WIDE CLASSROOM GUIDANCE* © 2007 MAR*CO PRODUCTS, INC. 1-800-448-2197	You saw a student writing bad words on the bathroom wall. *What would you do or say?* BYE, BYE, BULLY SITUATION CARD *SCHOOL-WIDE CLASSROOM GUIDANCE* © 2007 MAR*CO PRODUCTS, INC. 1-800-448-2197
A student in your class asks to borrow a pencil, then refuses to give it back. *What would you do or say?* BYE, BYE, BULLY SITUATION CARD *SCHOOL-WIDE CLASSROOM GUIDANCE* © 2007 MAR*CO PRODUCTS, INC. 1-800-448-2197	No one is sitting with the new student at lunch. *What could you say or do to help him/her feel better?* BYE, BYE, BULLY SITUATION CARD *SCHOOL-WIDE CLASSROOM GUIDANCE* © 2007 MAR*CO PRODUCTS, INC. 1-800-448-2197
Your friend is spreading a rumor about someone in your class. *What would you do or say?* BYE, BYE, BULLY SITUATION CARD *SCHOOL-WIDE CLASSROOM GUIDANCE* © 2007 MAR*CO PRODUCTS, INC. 1-800-448-2197	An older student takes your lunch money. *What would you do or say?* BYE, BYE, BULLY SITUATION CARD *SCHOOL-WIDE CLASSROOM GUIDANCE* © 2007 MAR*CO PRODUCTS, INC. 1-800-448-2197

You Are Invited To Stop By The Guidance Center

On

_____

During conference night from

_____PM — _____PM

Every child will be able to select a lollipop from the
Bye, Bye, Bullies tree,
test his or her bully prevention I.Q.,
and maybe win a prize!

Looking forward to seeing you there!

_____
COUNSELOR

Shining Star Guidance Program

GAME PLAN 4 FOR SCHOOL-WIDE GUIDANCE (DECEMBER)

WHO:

Students in grades K-6

WHAT: CARING CANDLES

PROGRAM IN ACTION:

This activity is presented to reinforce acts of kindness performed by students. *Caring Candles* are awarded to students who perform caring acts for their parents, friends, and/or neighbors. For each caring act, the students must have a witness' signature on a *Caring Candle Certificate.* When the certificate is returned to school, the student will receive a *Caring Candle* from his/her teacher to color and place in the hallway of the school.

WHEN:

Send home the *Caring Candles Instructions* with the students after they return from Thanksgiving break.

WHERE:

The students perform their acts of kindness at home or in their neighborhoods. They return the *Caring Candle Certificate* to their teacher. The teacher will complete the lines on the *Caring Candle* activity sheet, then give the sheet to the student to color. When the candle is colored, it may be displayed in the hallway outside the student's classroom.

HOW:

Reproduce the following:

- ☐ *Caring Candles Instructions* for each student (page 96)
- ☐ *Caring Candle* activity sheet for the students to color (page 97)

CARING CANDLES
INSTRUCTIONS

Please take time this month to help someone by performing an act of kindness. An example of an act of kindness might be helping your parents with a chore at home, assisting a neighbor or grandparent with a project, or helping another student at school.

When you help someone, have that person sign the *Caring Candle Certificate* at the bottom of this sheet. Then return it to your homeroom teacher, who will give you a *Caring Candle* to color.

We will look for lots of *Caring Candles* decorating our halls before Winter Break!

GAME PLAN 5 FOR SCHOOL-WIDE GUIDANCE (JANUARY)

WHO:

Students in grades 1-6

WHAT: ACADEMIC SHINING STARS AWARD ASSEMBLIES

PROGRAM IN ACTION:

Academic Shining Stars are awarded at the end of each school semester. The teachers nominate first-, second-, and third-graders based on the acquired skills needed to achieve good grades in the future. Fourth-, fifth-, and sixth-graders are recognized for the grades they receive on their report cards. There is an *Academic Excellence Certificate* for students who earn all *A's*, a *High Honor Roll* for students who earn all *A's and B's*, and a *Merit Roll* for students who earn *A's, B's, and C's.* Each qualifying student receives a certificate and a *Shining Star Wand* (see page 29). An alternate to a wand would be to give each student a stuffed star. (*Note*: The Oriental Trading Company [www.orientaltrading.com] has stuffed stars [Item number: IN-6/1247] available in six different colors. So you can assign each grade a color and the stars will not overlap from year to year.)

WHEN:

Select dates for two *Academic Shining Stars Assemblies* for the year. One should take place in late January or whenever your first semester ends, and the other should be held at the end of the school year. You may wish to have different assemblies for the older and younger children because of the short attention spans of the younger students.

Provide the teachers of first, second, and third grades with *Academic Responsibility Awards Nomination Forms* two weeks before your planned assembly and give fourth-, fifth-, and sixth-grade teachers *Academic Shining Stars Reporting Forms*. Ask the teachers to complete the forms and return them to you one week before your assembly. This will give you enough time to prepare the awards and certificates.

WHERE:

The assemblies can take place in your school's auditorium, gym, or other special place where you have enough room to assemble the number of children who will be attending. You may also wish to invite parents to be a part of your recognition assembly.

HOW:

Reproduce the following:

- ☐ *Academic Responsibility Awards Nomination Form* for teachers in Grades 1-3 (page 100)

- ☐ *Academic Shining Stars Reporting Form* for teachers in Grades 4-6 (page 101)

- ☐ *Certificate Of Academic Responsibility* for qualifying students (pages 102-106)

- ☐ *Academic Excellence Certificate* for qualifying students (page 107)

- ☐ *High Honor Roll Certificate* for qualifying students (page 108)

- ☐ *Merit Roll Certificate* for qualifying students (page 109)

Optional: purchase stuffed stars.

TEACHER'S NAME

_____

ACADEMIC RESPONSIBILITY AWARDS NOMINATION FORM

⭐ Best Listener _____

⭐ Most Responsible _____

⭐ Awesome Organizer _____

⭐ #1 Homework Completer _____

⭐ Fabulous Follower of Directions _____

Please nominate one student from your homeroom for each award. These awards will be given out on _____ in the _____. Thank you!

If you have any questions, please see _____ .

RETURN THE FORM BY _____ to _____

Shining Star Guidance Program

TEACHER'S NAME

_____

ACADEMIC
Shining Stars
REPORTING FORM

Please list the students in your homeroom who earned the following grades on their report cards, qualifying them for the following:

Academic Excellence (All *A's*)

_____   _____
_____   _____
_____   _____
_____   _____
_____   _____

High Honor Roll (All *A's* and *B's*)

_____   _____
_____   _____
_____   _____
_____   _____
_____   _____

Merit Roll (All *A's*, *B's*, and *C's*)

_____   _____
_____   _____
_____   _____
_____   _____
_____   _____

RETURN THE FORM BY _____ to _____

Shining Star Guidance Program

CERTIFICATE OF ACADEMIC RESPONSIBILITY

This certificate is awarded to

_____

in recognition for displaying the
MOST RESPONSIBLE BEHAVIOR

in _____'s class.

_____
GRADE

_____
DATE

_____
COUNSELOR'S NAME

Good Job!

CERTIFICATE OF ACADEMIC RESPONSIBILITY

This certificate is awarded to

_____

in recognition for being an
AWESOME ORGANIZER

in _____'s class.

_____
GRADE

_____
DATE

_____
COUNSELOR'S NAME

Good Job!

Shining Star Guidance Program

Shining Star Guidance Program

CERTIFICATE OF ACADEMIC RESPONSIBILITY

This certificate is awarded to

_____

in recognition for being the
#1 HOMEWORK COMPLETER

in _____'s class.

_____
GRADE

_____
DATE

_____
COUNSELOR'S NAME

Good Job!

Shining Star Guidance Program

CERTIFICATE OF ACADEMIC RESPONSIBILITY

This certificate is awarded to

_____

in recognition for being the
BEST LISTENER

in _____'s class.

_____
GRADE

_____
DATE

_____
COUNSELOR'S NAME

Good Job!

Shining Star Guidance Program

CERTIFICATE OF ACADEMIC RESPONSIBILITY

This certificate is awarded to

_____

in recognition for being a
**FABULOUS FOLLOWER
OF DIRECTIONS**

in _____'s class.

_____
GRADE

_____
DATE

_____
COUNSELOR'S NAME

Good Job!

Shining Star Guidance Program

ACADEMIC EXCELLENCE

THIS CERTIFICATE IS PRESENTED TO

_____

FOR RECEIVING ALL A's AT

_____
SCHOOL NAME

_____   _____
GRADE   DATE

_____
PRINCIPAL'S SIGNATURE

_____
TEACHER'S SIGNATURE

_____
COUNSELOR'S SIGNATURE

GAME PLAN 6 FOR SCHOOL-WIDE GUIDANCE (FEBRUARY)

WHO:

Students in grades K-5

WHAT: NATIONAL SCHOOL COUNSELORS' WEEK

PROGRAM IN ACTION:

Place the drawing cards and a container in the teachers' lounge. Distribute the *National School Counselors' Week Prize List* to each teacher. Teachers may enter the drawing to win: an extra classroom lesson, group pullout, video/DVD lesson, or book to be read to the class. At the end of the week, draw a selected number of lucky teachers' homerooms and announce them on your school's public address system. Then talk with each teacher to set up a convenient time to present his/her prize.

WHEN:

This special week in February is the ideal time to remind your staff and students about your role as school counselor and how you contribute to the students' general health and wellbeing. Introduce it by giving each teacher a copy of *It's National School Counselors' Week*.

WHERE:

The drawing takes place in the teachers' lounge and the lessons are presented in the winning teachers' homerooms.

HOW:

Reproduce the following:

- ☐ *It's National School Counselors' Week* for each teacher (page 111)
- ☐ *It's National School Counselors' Week* drawing cards, one for each teacher (page 112)
- ☐ *It's National School Counselors' Week* prize list for each teacher (page 113)

Collect videos/DVDs, books, and educational lessons to be used as prizes

IT'S NATIONAL SCHOOL COUNSELORS' WEEK

Did you know that your school counselor provides the following services?

- Classroom Guidance Lessons

- Small-Group Counseling Sessions

- Parent Workshops

- *Shining Stars* Recognition Program

- *Word Of The Month* Activities

- Response To Individual Referrals By Students, Teachers, And Parents

IT'S NATIONAL SCHOOL COUNSELORS' WEEK

TEACHER'S NAME _____

GRADE LEVEL _____

I PREFER A:
- [ ] Group pullout on _____
- [ ] Classroom lesson
- [ ] Book lesson read to my class
- [ ] Video/DVD lesson

IF I WIN!

IT'S NATIONAL SCHOOL COUNSELORS' WEEK

TEACHER'S NAME _____

GRADE LEVEL _____

I PREFER A:
- [ ] Group pullout on _____
- [ ] Classroom lesson
- [ ] Book lesson read to my class
- [ ] Video/DVD lesson

IF I WIN!

IT'S NATIONAL SCHOOL COUNSELORS' WEEK

Please enter the drawing to win

BIG PRIZES

to benefit you and your students!

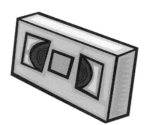

YOU COULD WIN A:

Classroom Lesson
Video/DVD Classroom Lesson
Book Read To The Class
Group Pullout

Good Luck!

GAME PLAN 7 FOR SCHOOL-WIDE GUIDANCE (MARCH)

WHO:

Students in grades K-6

WHAT: IN YOUR OWN WORDS...

PROGRAM IN ACTION:

This program gives students the opportunity to tell what selected character traits or *Words Of The Month* mean to them and to receive school-wide recognition.

The first decision to be made is whether you want to use one word or several for the month. Depending upon your decision, reproduce the *In Your Own Words...* handouts and distribute them to each student. After the handouts have been returned to you, select those that you wish to read school-wide. During morning announcements each day, read one statement to the entire school. Announce the student's name and grade. You might wish to have the students, themselves, read their work. Each lucky reader could also receive a small gift such as a pencil with the word described printed on it.

WHEN:

Distribute the handouts to all students at the end of the month. Tell them to write one or two sentences describing what the specified word means to them. Collect the handouts and read one, or have one read, during morning announcements the following month.

WHERE:

Announcements are read from the main office each morning.

HOW:

Reproduce the following:

☐ *In Your Own Words...* for each student (pages 115-120)

Optional: Prizes for the students chosen to read.

In Your Own Words...
How can you show other people that you care about them?

_____

_____

_____

_____

NAME _____ GRADE ____

TEACHER _____

In Your Own Words...
How can you be a good citizen?

_____

_____

_____

_____

NAME _____ GRADE ____

TEACHER _____

In Your Own Words...
How can you show that you have confidence in what you are doing?

_____

_____

_____

_____

NAME _____ GRADE _____

TEACHER _____

In Your Own Words...
What does it mean *to cooperate with other people?*

_____

_____

_____

_____

NAME _____ GRADE _____

TEACHER _____

In Your Own Words...
How do you show that you are a courageous person?

_____

_____

_____

_____

NAME _____ GRADE _____

TEACHER _____

In Your Own Words...
What does it mean *to play fairly*?

_____

_____

_____

_____

NAME _____ GRADE _____

TEACHER _____

In Your Own Words...
How do you show that you are an honest person?

_____

_____

_____

_____

NAME _____ GRADE _____

TEACHER _____

In Your Own Words...
What does it mean *to persevere?*

_____

_____

_____

_____

NAME _____ GRADE _____

TEACHER _____

In Your Own Words...
How do you show respect to other people?

_____

_____

_____

_____

NAME _____ GRADE _____

TEACHER _____

In Your Own Words...
What does it mean *to be responsible?*

_____

_____

_____

_____

NAME _____ GRADE _____

TEACHER _____

In Your Own Words...
How do you show that you are a tolerant person?

_____

_____

_____

_____

NAME _____ GRADE _____

TEACHER _____

In Your Own Words...
What does *work ethic* mean?

_____

_____

_____

_____

NAME _____ GRADE _____

TEACHER _____

GAME PLAN 8 FOR SCHOOL-WIDE GUIDANCE
(APRIL)

WHO:

Students in grades K-6

WHAT: DUCKY DAYS (A JUST-FOR-FUN ACTIVITY)

PROGRAM IN ACTION:

We often reward kids for doing well, making good grades, or excelling at a certain task. But we must realize that all kids need to be recognized and appreciated and made to feel special. This is the goal for *Ducky Days*. The students who find the hidden ducks may be children you have never really talked with or don't even know. This is their time to feel special and get to know the counselor! Kids will look forward to this activity all year long.

On the morning announcements the day before *Ducky Day*, describe what will take place. Say something like:

> Tomorrow is *Ducky Day*. This means that approximately 20-30 ducks have been hidden all over the school. If you are a student in Grades K through 6 and you find a duck, please bring it to the counselor's office at 2 o'clock tomorrow to pick up your prize. Happy hunting!

Repeat the announcement the day of *Ducky Day* the following morning, changing the word *tomorrow* to *today*.

WHEN:

Schedule the activity a day or two before Spring Break begins, when the students are getting antsy and need a project that requires them to use their thinking skills.

WHERE:

Hide the ducks all over the school the night before *Ducky Day*. Alert the teachers and staff of your intentions.

HOW:

Reproduce the following:

☐ *Staff Alert For Ducky Day!* for each teacher and staff member (page 123)

Purchase *Rubber Duckys* (order from the Oriental Trading Co., www.orientaltrading.com, item number: IN-16/842) or make little ducks from the provided pattern (see page 124).

Collect prizes that will make students think about gearing up for Spring Break. Examples could be towels, sand buckets, inexpensive games, edible treats, tickets to the local movie theater or skating rink, etc.

Staff Alert For Ducky Day!

Tomorrow is Ducky Day.
Be prepared to have fun!

Please send the lucky "duck" finders
to the guidance office at ___ p.m.

DUCK PATTERN

124

SCHOOL-WIDE GUIDANCE: BE A SHINING STAR! © 2007 MAR*CO PRODUCTS, INC. 1-800-448-2197

GAME PLAN 9 FOR SCHOOL-WIDE GUIDANCE (MAY)

WHO:

Students in grades 1-6

WHAT: MAY MAIL

PROGRAM IN ACTION:

During your final classroom guidance lesson or sometime during the month when you are not presenting classroom guidance, have the students think of a teacher in your school who influenced them or whom they really liked. Have each one complete a *May Mail* card for that teacher. The only rule is that they may not choose their current homeroom teacher—or else you would have all the students selecting that teacher and not really thinking about who made a difference to them. Make sure to let the students know that they may select any teachers of special subjects as well as classroom teachers.

When the students have completed their cards, collect the cards to be distributed through the teachers' mailboxes at a later time. What a way to end the year! Teachers get very excited about receiving "Thank yous," especially from children, and this warm feeling will extend to you and your counseling program!

WHEN:

Schedule the activity for the last month of school.

WHERE:

Have the students complete the cards during your final classroom visit of the year. Collect the cards when they have finished.

HOW:

Reproduce the following:

- ☐ *Thank You* cards for each student (pages 126-128). Fold the cards in half, then in half again to make greeting cards.

Shining Star

GREETINGS

MAR*CO PRODUCTS, INC.

Shining Star

GREETINGS

MAR*CO PRODUCTS, INC.

Thank You

Shining Star

GREETINGS

MAR*CO PRODUCTS, INC.